HACKING

A Beginners Guide To Your F.
Learn To Crack A Wireless Network, Basic Security
Penetration Made Easy and Step By Step Kali Linux

I0019754

Descrierea CIP a Bibliotecii Naţionale a României
WHITE, KEVIN

    Hacking. A Beginners Guide To Your First Computer Hack
Learn To Crack A Wireless Network, Basic Security Penetration
Made Easy and Step By Step Kali Linux / by Kevin White. -
Bucureşti : My Ebook, 2018
    ISBN 978-606-983-600-2

004

HACKING

A Beginners Guide To Your First Computer Hack
Learn To Crack A Wireless Network, Basic Security
Penetration Made Easy and Step By Step Kali Linux

My Ebook Publishing House
Bucharest, 2018

CONTENTS

Introduction

I want to thank you and congratulate you for buying the book, *"Hacking: A Beginners Guide To Your First Computer Hack; Learn To Crack A Wireless Network, Basic Security Penetration Made Easy and Step By Step Kali Linux"*.

This book contains proven steps and strategies on how to hack a Wireless Network, carry out a penetration test and protect yourself and company from hackers and so much more. It also gives an insight to the activities of hackers and ways to counter their attacks.

Thanks again for purchasing this book, I hope you enjoy it!

This document is geared towards providing exact and reliable information in regards to the topic and issue covered. The publication is sold with the idea that the publisher is not required to render accounting, officially permitted, or otherwise, qualified services. If advice is necessary, legal or professional, a practiced individual in the profession should be ordered.

- From a Declaration of Principles which was accepted and approved equally by a Committee of the American Bar Association and a Committee of Publishers and Associations.

In no way is it legal to reproduce, duplicate, or transmit any part of this document in either electronic means or in printed format. Recording of this publication is strictly prohibited and any storage of this document is not allowed unless with written permission from the publisher. All rights reserved.

The information provided herein is stated to be truthful and consistent, in that any liability, in terms of

Chapter 1

What is Hacking?

Computers are very useful in most of our daily affairs; it has often been tagged a necessity for the success of any business. Most companies have their private data or corporate data stored up somewhere or being transferred over the internet and lead to exposure to cyber criminals who are out to exploit them through a process known as Hacking. The knowledge of hacking can help protect businesses and individuals from these attacks.

Hacking is a way of accessing a computers privacy or network system with the aim of altering its behaviour and functions. Prior to this times, hacking has always had a positive meaning used to describe intellectual, smart, technical approach to computer solutions. Hacking involves taking advantage of the computers weakness to access vital information on the computer.

Hacking and cracking mean different things. Most of the malicious attacks usually attributed to hacking are formally known as cracking and this has overshadowed the positive aspects of hacking. This distinction is hardly found outside the technical field, as everything that threatens the security of computer is generally termed Hacking.

A person who identifies weak points in a computer and network system with the sole aim of gaining access is known as a Hacker.

Everyone has the right to privacy, and this simply means that you are in charge of the amount of information you give out about yourself. With the use of the internet, some information about you are stuck on different servers for websites you must have accessed. It is important you protect yourself against fraudulent individuals, cyber criminals, and malicious agents before you get into trouble. Hackers can have this access because of the internet without considering properly the privacy of internet users. You can also describe Hacking as a way of protecting your right to privacy.

The process of hacking started with good intentions, but now it has mostly been associated with negative activities such as Identity theft, credit card theft, and all others. What comes to mind when the word hacking is said is always negative especially to a novice in the field. No doubt, hacking has been used to commit a lot of crimes on websites, network and some other commercial fields, hacking has also been used in discovering loop holes in a system a preventing a lot of these crimes as well.

There are security specialist whose job is to counter the attacks of these cyber criminals. Many more have been done by these specialists in preventing malicious attacks than has been said. They are known as the Whitehats while the others in the other category are called the Blackhats, both possessing the same level of knowledge and skill on computer affairs while the Whitehats decides to uses this knowledge positively they are using it the other way round. Softwares usually have loop holes they both look for these holes with one aiming at averting the problems that will arise from the lapses and the other (blackhats) trying to take advantage of the loopholes at the detriment of the user.

Hacking like every other technical stuff will demand your full dedication and interest and also a desire and a craving for knowledge and advancement. If your goal is to be a hacker, prepare to be dedicated.

What kind of hacker would you like to be? Make your choice from the options below. Hackers are usually qualified based on their hacking goals.

Script Kiddie

Script Kiddies refers to those who have no intention of learning from any hacking job done. They are neither innovative nor creative. They are simply satisfied with discovering the tricks used by hackers and doing nothing else but that. They are only capable of undertaking tasks that involve repeating processes used by others, even though they familiarise themselves with tools created by others they would do nothing to create their own tool. Be better than a script kiddie.

Black hat

These are the trouble makers, who are only interested in exploiting people for selfish reasons such as greed, hate and even to show off their skills. They are involved in all types of cyber crimes ranging from stealing data and identities to credit card information and money. They are the reason lots of money is being used up today for sustaining cyber security. Viruses, Malware, and Trojans serve as in roads to the user's computers through which these hackers operate. Don't be a blackhat hacker.

White hat

White hat hackers are the angels whose actions are solely backed up by good intentions. They are directed at enhancing system security through hacking. One of the ways through which they do this is by Penetration testing. Penetration testing involve saccessing a system for loop holes, lapses or vulnerability and patching them up before the blackhat guys come along the same route to exploit them. Since the hacking process is the same for the both guys, they are most likely going to be discovering vulnerabilities. It now depends on who gets there first. More people are picking interest in the field of Software security and has resulted in its massive growth. There is a lot of room for you in the field of cyber security. Don't miss out on this one.

Grey hat hackers

These are the hackers whose actions are driven by the situation at hand. They are not known for being either positive or negative. They do things mostly for fun irrespective of what it is. They also engage in the search for vulnerabilities in a system with no intent of exploiting it but for the fame or thrill that goes with it. In a bid to do this, they often violate the law because the law frowns at anything that has to do with invading a systems privacy.

Hacktivists

Hacktivists are social hackers who fights against injustice and uphold the rights of individuals through their hacking skills. They use their hacking skills to get their voice heard; they may attack a website to get supporters for a particular case that has been treated unfairly. They are concerned about the interest of the people and do not mind using their skills to pursue this interest. This though positive may sometimes violate the law. They sometimes carry out illegal actions to get their voice heard. It is their own way of delivering justice. Renowned hacktivits includes Wikileaks, LulzSec.

Which of the categories have you considered worth belonging to? Still indifferent? Bear in mind that hacking follows the same process in all the categories, but the intent is what makes the different. Where will you channel all the efforts too?

Also remember that it involves being practical, less theory more practical!

But before we can do that, let's get you all set up with a virtual machine so that you don't accidentally wreck your computer. Safety first, right?

Chapter 2

Hacking A Wireless Network

A wireless network is a network used to connect two or more devices or computers. It makes use of radio waves. It is done at the physical layer of the OSI model.

Wireless Network Authentication

With the wireless network turned on any device can connect to any available wireless network. Wireless networks are easily accessible to any device within its reach, and it is for this reason that most wireless networks come with a password to prevent free access. Authentication techniques which are commonly used are the WEP and the WPA

WEP

WEP stands for Wired Equivalent Privacy. It is targeted at providing a privacy level that is similar to the wire network privacy. It secures data by encryption as passes through the internet, to keep it safe from intruders. The IEEE 802.11 WLAN standards brought about its existence.

WEP Authentication

Open System Authentication (OSA) – this method is determined by the laid down access policy. WEP with the OSA only grants access to station authentication requesting if it matches the configured policy.

Shared Key Authentication (SKA) – in this method, an encrypted challenge is sent to station, the station then responds by encrypting its key with the challenge. The system now checks if the encrypted challenge in the response corresponds with the AP value.

WEP Vulnerability

The flaws and lapses of WEP are listed below

1. The tool used to check the integrity of the packets is the Cyclic Redundancy Check (CRC32). This tool is not good enough because the contents of the packets can be altered after capturing two packets. Though these bits are encrypted, the attacker may modify the encrypted packet so it is not rejected. This leads to unauthorized access to the network.

2. WEP makes use of stream ciphers which are created by the RC4 encryption algorithm to create stream ciphers. The stream cipher input consists of an (IV) initial value and a secret key. The initial value has a total length of 24 bits while the secret key has a length of

40 and 104 bits. Following this, the total length of the stream cipher created is either64 bits or 128 bits long. For an increased security level, keep a higher security key. They are usually more difficult to crack.

3. Keys management system is decentralized making the WEP not that flexible on larger networks. Try to change your keys using a WEP on a large network will give you a clearer view of how difficult it can be.

4. Weak Initial values as well as the lower secret keys are usually poorly encrypted when sent and this increases their vulnerability to cyber crimes.

5. Dictionary attacks can easily be done on WEP because it makes use of passwords

These flaws in the WEP initiated the building of the WPA.

WPA

The acronym WPA stands for Wi-Fi Protected Access. The Wi-Fi Alliance created it to fill up the loop holes found in the WEP. It also encrypts data like the WEP, but its initial value doubles that of WEP. Unlike the WEP where keys can be reused for encrypting packets, WPA only uses temporal keys.

WPA Weaknesses

1. Denial of service can gain quick access to the system. Pre-shared keys use passphrases.
2. The collision avoidance implementation maybe altered.
3. Passphrases which are used for WPA are also vulnerable to dictionary attacks.

Wireless Network Hacking:

Cracking Wireless network WEP/WPA keys

WEP and WPA keys that determine the accessibility of any wireless network. Cracking this network types for access is possible especially when the network of interest is very active. It is more difficult to crack inactive networks. Cracking these softwares have been made possible with the availability of softwares and hardware resources such as Metasploit, Ophcrack, Wireshark, Aircrack-ng, and others. Patience is also required for the cracking process.

How to Crack Wireless Networks

WEP Cracking

Cracking involves taking advantage of the computers security weakness in wireless networks to access vital information on the computer. Two main types of cracking exist:

1. *Passive cracking* which does not affect the network traffic until the cracking of the WEP taken place.   Detecting this cracking involves tedious efforts

2. *Active cracking* can be easily detected. It greatly affects the network traffic by increasing the load effect. It a more effective way of cracking WEP.

WEP Cracking Tools

1. *Aircrack* – You will need to download WEP cracker and network sniffer to enable you eavesdrop on network activies.

2. *WEP Crack* – this is an effective way of breaking 802.11 WEP secret keys. It is an open source implementation of the FMS attack

3. *Kismet-* includes detecting both the hidden and the visible, available wireless and intrusions as well as sniffer packets.

4. *Web Decrypt* – this tool cracks WEP keys through dictionary attacks. It sometimes generates its keys using a key generator. It has also been known to implement packets.

WPA Cracking

In a WPA system, authentication is done using a passphrase or pre-shared keys. While using passphrase use longer ones that are not prone to attacks created for cracking passwords such as dictionary attacks. One of the tools used for cracking the WPA keys is the Cow patty. *Cow Patty uses the brute force attack for cracking Pre-sharedkey*s.

There are other types of authentications that can be used with WPA/WPA2 apart from pre-shared keys. Aircrack-ng is specialised for cracking pre-shared keys. So confirm if the authentication type of the network is PSK, you can use airodump-ng for the confirmation. Once again because other network types are uncrackable with Aircrack-ng. Even if you don't confirm you may be lucky to be working with a network type of PSK because that's what most networks use. It is a goof practice to confirm first.

It is only possible to crack the pre-shared key if the word is relatively short and if it can be found in a dictionary. That is why it is advisable to use a password as long as 63 characters, having random characters and symbols. This is because hacking using the dictionary attack involves testing everyone in a text file to determine if it is the password. It also involves using the "Dictionary attack list" which provides all known words of varying lenth in a text file. Each word in the file is tested to identify the password.

The approach used for cracking WPA/WPA2 and WEP are different. This is a big distinction in their cracking process. In the cracking of WEP, the speed of the cracking process can be increased using statistical methods while the WPA/WPA2 is cracked using the plain brute force techniques only. Information about when to begin an attack is indicated by the handshake between the AP and the client. Another reason why the pre-shared key is difficult to crack is that the password ranges for 8-63 characters, it is, therefore, difficult to determine especially in cases where unusual passwords are set. Brute-force finds it difficult to crack an eight character password.

In other words, if the dictionary does not contain the passphrase then aircrack-ng will not be able to crack it.

General mode of attack

1. *Sniffing*, as the name implies, captures encrypted data as they are being transferred over a network. This data can then be decoded using other cracking tools.

2. *Man in the Middle (MITM) Attack* pays close attention to a network while searching for sensitive information. Once it senses a desired information, it captures it.

3. *Denial of Service Attack* – This attack prevents users from getting access to network resources.

How to secure wireless networks

To reduce the number or frequency of network attacks, you will need to

i. Create new passwords for the hardware and disable the others.

ii. Get an authentication mechanism running.

iii. Restrict network access by using a MAC address.

iv. Enable your firewall.

v. Create strong passwords for WEP and WPA-PSK keys with a character length of about 63 that combines numbers, characters, and symbols. This way it will not be easily cracked using brute force and dictionary attacks. Only relative short PSK's can be cracked easily. A password as long as 63 characters work well against dictionary attacks because cracking it will be quite tedious.

Chapter 3

Kali Linux

Linux is an open source server operating system. Some of the Linux based operating systems are the Ubuntu, Redhat etc. It is widely used over the internet. Everyone has access to the underlying source code. Thereby making itmore vulnerable to cyberattacks. Since the source code is easily accessible, crackers look out for the weakness in the system and can easily exploit it. These form the basis for hacking Kali Linux systems.

Kali Linux was designed by the Debianlinux distribution for penetration testing and digital forensics. It imports most of the packages used to run the system from Debian repositories.

Only a small number of people are involved in developing Kali Linux system. These people must be trusted and reliable to be part of the Linux team. Package development is usually done with the use of a secure environment. After development, the developer digitally endorses the package with a signature. The development team working with Kali Linux systems discovered the need for carrying out wireless assessment, so they introduced the custom built kernel patched specifically for 802.11 wireless injection.

Linux carries out server functions; it also functions as an operating system in mobile devices, tablets, and desktops

GUI and command are used in operating Linux programs. GUI's are not as effective as the commands. The use of commands also familiarises the user with basic Linux commands.

Linux Hacking Tools

Nessus: Configuration settings, networks scanning is done using this tool.

NMap: Details of the host present on a server and the tools they use can be extracted using the NMap.

SARA (Security Auditor's Research Assistant): SARA can be used to scan networks in order to protect them against threats such as XSS and SQL injection.

Several other tools that can be used for hacking Linux systems still exists.

How to prevent Linux hacks

Linux Hackers exploits the weakness in its operating system. If you are concerned about preventing hackers attack, then the methods listed below will be of help.

Patch management – Bugs serve as an entrance point to attacks. Hackers exploit these bugs to gain access to a system. Patches do the job of fixing these bugs. Applying patches to fix bugs is what is involved in patch management. For effective protection, fix patches as often as possible.

Proper OS configuration – if the server is not properly configured, it could serve as a weakness to the network of for hackers to exploits. Default settings should be changed from time to time as well as port numbers. The server should eliminate any unnecessary information available such as inactive usernames.

Intrusion Detection System – this tool detects the presence of an attack on a system. This tool specializes in detecting unwanted access to a system while some other tools can both detect and prevent attacks.

Chapter 4

Penetration Test

A penetration test is an attack performed on a system to determine the system security level. The pen test as it is also known is done to discover vulnerabilities to an attack from unauthorised parties trying to gain access to system's data. Penetration testing starts from identifying the devices(boundary rooters, firewalls, servers, switches)that exist within your environment. After determining the availability of this device, you can decide the plan of the network. Following this is the testing of the different system and devices for vulnerability spots using hacker's tools and methods. You will also need to check if the system will be affected by possible attacks with vulnerability scans, denial of service attacks. Playing the hackers' role, you will need tools like PING to identify live host, and ports open on devices to keep track of what these devices are used for.

In summary, penetration testing aims at discovering vulnerabilities in devices under a network and making sure they are patched to prevent access from an unwanted external body. It gives an idea of how secure your network is from a hacker's point of view.

Why is Penetration testing important?

With the increase in the number of hacking making the news headlines, it is important that we protect ourselves from these hackers. Hackers take their time in making sure they search and discover weaknesses in computer systems. These weaknesses are sometimes attributed to bad coding. They may include bugs, application back doors, spy ware penetrated application codes, operating system at the time the application or product were produced which have now been replaced in the form of viruses or Trojans. We can protect ourselves by discovering our systems vulnerabilities first and exploiting it for ways to protect the system before these hackers exploit it negatively.

Hackers have been known to use DOS attacks on reputable companies such as banks, ISPs. They do all these things fro various reasons ranging from selfishness to vengeance on a company they were denied employment or even to gain popularity in their field.

Companies who create systems receive alerts of new vulnerabilities, individuals too may become conscious of vulnerabilities through the efforts of Computer Emergency Response Team (CERT) andmany other CERT's who compile new vulnerabilities and publish them to companies as well as security companies to either harden the system in the area of weakness or perhaps create patches for them.

Penetration testing should be done constantly and repeated to check for other available routes through which unauthorized operations can be performed.

Who should perform Penetration testing?

Penetration testing can be done directly by employing the help of auditing systems to be in charge of the testing. Some companies are looking forward to having a team who will be carrying out constant check for vulnerabilities on the device and also look out for publications from CERT and then prepare a relevant patch for this weakness that matches accordingly.

Anyone who is well informed and updated in the latest attack mechanism, penetration applications and is well trained with convincing experience or perhaps is certified in that field.

Not everyone or company that goes by the name penetration tester should be employed to avoid employing a hacker who does not have your interest at heart. Ensure that they have been certified by security personnel, that they have liability insurance and their hackers work with the company's agenda.

Specialized OS distributions

Kali Linux, Parrot Security, Pentoo operating systems were created to serve for penetration testing purposes. These are not exhaustive; other operating systems support penetration testing too. Some operating systems are mlre specialised focusing more on an aspect of penetration testing. Operating systems like Damn Vulnerable Linux (DVL), and the metasploitable can be used as targets for trying new security tools, especially in a lab environment especially by security professionals new to the field.

Once the attacker has exploited one vulnerability, they may gain access to other machines, so the process repeats, i.e. look for new vulnerabilities and attempt to exploit them. This process is referred to as pivoting.

Creating the Penetration Test Kit

Test Environment

Penetration testing should be carried out in a lab environment. This hacking test can lead to destruction of systems and are very dangerous especially of you have to use hacking tools. It is for this reason that setting up a test environment is advised. You can set up a test environment by simply connecting multiple devices with a network set up. Ensure you have an updated antivirus installed. Download the required tools then check for the presence of a Trojan virus which is the most common. Most of these downloads usually come with Trojan virus within the installation.

Hardware

For your penetration test kit, you will need three to four PCs. Each of them having a speed of above

250 MHz with a large ram that will accommodate multiple applications as you have in a real situation. With virtual machines, you can get a feel of a computer environment from a software perspective and operating system while carrying out your test. Virtual machines permit for multiple workstations and servers to be accessed without using the main network and server.

Virtual machines also give room for corrections in cases where the system crashes. You can undo changes after a crash, the virtual machine provides an option for discarding changes made to the machine since the last time the system was started. This option is displayed after the system has been powered off and then on again.

Operating Systems

Most of the security tools used for penetration testing are on the Linux and Windows platforms (more recent). Without a basic knowledge of these two operating systems, it would be difficult to carry out a successful penetration test. You will need a basic fundamental knowledge of both Linux and Windows. You should be able to install software, configure it, create operating systems, log in as an administrator and configure hardware too.

Researching Security tools

There are just a few of security tools used for penetration test available on the internet. Searching and searching will only bring a more updated version because they are updated as soon as a weakness is noticed. Most likely because most people search for them or even because they are free. Now this means that the hackers might be using them too. These tools make penetration testing easier and faster because the bring pen test closer to being automated.

Recommended Tools for research

Some of the tools used for pen test are the Redhat 7.2 Enimga, Linux, Trinux, Nmap.

Chapter 5

Your First Hack: WEP Network

Before starting you will need to download some tools. The Comm View for WiFi from http://tamos.com/download/main/ca.php, Aircarck-NG GUI fromhttp://aircrack-ng.org/ and also a virtual environment like we discussed in the last chapter. To avoid directly affecting your system.

While installing the CommView, you will be asked to choose between installing the application in Standard mode or the VoIP mode. You can select any of them till you develop a preference for any of them. Once the option is taken, the drivers required to enable the wireless adapter for capturing packet data are automatically installed after it must have completed the search process. When the installation is done, CommView disables the WIFI connection.

When the application is fully started, on the left side, you will find a left arrow. Click on it. Then it displays a new window with the start scanning button. On click, the system scans for available networks and displays them in the right column. Click on the network whose password you seek to get, and then "Capture." On click, the opened windows close while CommView captures packets.

Go to the options in the setting menu, then look for memory usage enter a value of 20000 for the maximum packets in buffer.

Also, go to "Auto logging" in the logging tab, set the "Maximum Directory Size" to 2000 and the "Average Log File Size" to 20. This step signals CommView that each .ncp packets should have a file size of20MB and be stored in the desired directory.

Select the "logging" tab, then click on "Concatenate logs". By activating concatenate all the individual captured .ncp packet file will be combined into a single large file.

From the file menu, Go to "Load CommView Logs" after which we select the newly formed concatenated .ncf file.

From the file menu again, Export then click on Wireshark/Tco dump format. The .cap file is created after clicking.

Remember you downloaded the Aircrack application at the beginning. It is for this moment. So locate the Aircrack application folder and then locate the bin file. Still in a folder, double click on Aircrack-ng GUI.exe file, then select the newly created .cap file.

Selecting the .cap file should give you the password except in cases where you did not receive enough packets. A minimum of 10000 packets is required to start the cracking process. To avoid making a mistake, leave the system for a longer period of time before proceeding to the next step. And that's how to crack WEP passwords.

CommView is no longer free and its quite expensive too but you can also use other tools like the WireShark, to obtain the .cap file following the same steps. All the different tools can be used to extract the passwords.

Conclusion

Thank you again for purchasing this book!

I hope this book was able to help you to start your Hacking career.

The next step is to go ahead and practice and also keep learning. Remember, to be a successful hacker you need to have a craving for knowledge and learning.

Finally, if you enjoyed this book, then I'd like to ask you for a favor, would you be kind enough to leave a review for this book? It'd be greatly appreciated!

Thank you and good luck!